Disney

Pencils, Pens & Brushes

A Great Girls' Guide to Disney Animation

Written by **Mindy Johnson**

Illustrated by **Lorelay Bové**

Disney PRESS

LOS ANGELES · NEW YORK

For Dreamers in search of their Greatness!

—MJ

Cheers to all the Ladies that made history in Disney Animation Studios and that inspired and keep inspiring other generations! And to the wishful thinkers and visionaries!

—LB

Designed by Winnie Ho

Copyright © 2019 Disney Enterprises, Inc.

All rights reserved. Published by Disney Press, an imprint of Disney Book Group. No part of this book may be reproduced or transmitted in any form or by any means, electronic or mechanical, including photocopying, recording, or by any information storage and retrieval system, without written permission from the publisher. For information address Disney Press, 1200 Grand Central Avenue, Glendale, California 91201.

Printed in Malaysia

First Hardcover Edition, August 2019

10 9 8 7 6 5 4 3 2 1

FAC-029191-19137

Library of Congress Control Number: 2018955233

ISBN 978-1-368-02868-4

Visit disneybooks.com

All girls are Great Girls!

Everyone is special, with their own interests, talents, and abilities. Throughout history, Great Girls have accomplished many exciting things, but somehow their stories are rarely told.

Some of the best artists in the world applied their talents to create Walt Disney's animated films. The Great Girls explored within these pages are a few of the hundreds of women who were part of the Walt Disney Studios from the 1920s through the 1950s. With typewriters, pencils, pens, brushes, and more, the different talents of these women brought Walt Disney's animation—from early black-and-white shorts through feature-length color films—to life.

Many of these Great Girls also did remarkable things in addition to their time with Disney Studios. From aviation to opera, chemistry to dance, their accomplishments knew no bounds. It wasn't always easy for these Great Girls, but they each found a way to work hard, overcome difficulties, and achieve their dreams.

So turn the page to learn more about the work and inspiring lives of these

Great Girls
of Walt Disney Animation!

Lillian & Edna

The Mrs. Disneys

We've heard about the Mr. Disneys (Walt and Roy), but do you know about the Mrs. Disneys? Lillian and Edna were the Great Girls who helped the Disney brothers achieve success.

After finishing college, Lillian Bounds moved from Idaho to Hollywood to start her career. "The Disneys were going to hire another girl to do the inking and painting [on their films]," remembered Lillian. She got the job! Walt Disney was a creative dreamer, while his brother Roy managed the business. Everyone in the tiny Disney Brothers Cartoon Studio helped make

each short film in the Alice Comedy series. "When he started taking me home from work," Lillian remembered, "I began to look at him like he was somebody." Soon Lillian and Walt fell in love.

Edna Francis met Roy Disney in Kansas City when her brother and Roy took Edna and her sister to a dance. "Roy had only two dance lessons," Edna remembered, "and he wasn't very good." Edna and Roy began dating and continued to write to each other after Roy moved to Los Angeles. With the success of the Disney brothers' Alice cartoon series, Roy sent for Edna to come to Hollywood so they could be married.

Lillian and Edna helped make the Disney Brothers Cartoon Studio a success. As Walt improved his animated cartoons, the little studio often ran short on cash. Lillian would save her paychecks so the brothers could meet their bills. Edna also made big meals for the artists who were working late into the evening, and helped paint the cels for the early Alice cartoons.

When Walt was planning his new animated series featuring a mouse named "Mortimer," Lillian had a very wise note: "I said it didn't sound very good," she laughed. She came up with the name Mickey. And oh boy, did it stick!

During the development of the first Mickey and Minnie cartoon, everyone helped out. "Edna and I filled in celluloid," said Lillian. "We worked day and night." Together, these Great Girls inked and painted over thirteen thousand cels to finish the film. "I just tried to do it as best I could!" laughed Edna. Two more Mickey and Minnie cartoons were made before everyone's favorite mice became famous with *Steamboat Willie* in 1928.

Throughout their lives together, Lillian and Edna supported Walt and Roy as the Disney brothers continued to tell entertaining stories and create magical lands for everyone around the world to enjoy!

Supportive and *smart* in all that they do,

Great Girls stick with it and see things through.

Dorothy Ann Blank

(1901–1957)

Writer Extraordinaire

What stories do you want to tell? A Great Girl named Dorothy Ann Blank wrote some of the happiest tales ever told.

Walt Disney was expanding his animation studio. His Mickey Mouse cartoons were very popular and his Silly Symphonies series had become a big success! In order to bring new story ideas to the screen, Walt brought a successful writer for early movie magazines named Dorothy Ann Blank to the Disney Studios, where she founded the Story Development Department.

Dorothy's job was to explore how different tales could become animated movies; Walt had one at the top of the list: "Snow White." Dorothy made a plan and went to work, figuring out just how the story of Snow White could be told through animation. She asked herself questions such as: *What characters could be included in this story? What would they look like? What time and place would this story begin? What would the world look like? What would each character say? How would the story be entertaining for audiences?*

These questions needed answers before Walt and his artists could begin. To find them, Dorothy wrote different versions of Snow White's story, adding different characters and changing the order of the scenes to make Walt's fairy tale enchanting and memorable.

Once she had the elements she liked, Dorothy created a story map for the Animators. She described all the characters in detail—how they looked and acted in each scene. She wrote all the words that each character would say. Finally, she listed all the scenes to piece the story together in a dramatic and funny way. Now Walt Disney's artists could draw, animate, ink, and paint—and create their first hand-painted animated feature film, *Snow White and the Seven Dwarfs*!

Dorothy was such an important part of telling the story of *Snow White* that the artists at the Studio even modeled the Queen after her as a tribute! She was also the first woman to receive a credit for writing a Disney feature-length animated film and established a process for how animated stories could be told. Even today, animated films at Disney Studios are researched and written in the same way Dorothy Ann Blank told her stories.

To tell

great

stories

as best as you can,

start like

Dorothy

and draft a plan.

Nelbert Chouinard

(1879–1967)

Teaching Artists to Dream

Have you ever let someone believe in your dreams, too? When Nelbert Chouinard believed in helping someone's dream come true, this Great Girl changed an art form forever!

Young Nelbert Murphy had a curious mind. Growing up in Minnesota, Nelbert loved art. She painted and sketched all that she saw, dreaming of sharing her creativity with others. As she grew, Nelbert's artistry grew, too. She traveled to Brooklyn, New York, where she studied at the prestigious Pratt Institute. Nelbert became a fine painter and sculptor, but she wanted to share her love of art, so she began to teach others to express themselves through creativity, too.

Nelbert continued to study many art forms, teaching in New Jersey and El Paso, Texas. There, she married and became Mrs. Chouinard. Sadly, Nelbert's husband passed away during World War I, so she moved to California, where she established her very own school. Painters, sculptors, illustrators, filmmakers, fashion designers, and graphic artists all trained to become the finest artists in the world at the Chouinard Art Institute.

To Nelbert, everyone had a spark inside that only needed the right education to be ignited. With the tools and experiences she provided her

students, they learned to see the world through an artist's eye, and to be fearless with their art—with no limits or boundaries. Nelbert also mentored young artists and granted many scholarships to help her students achieve their dreams.

One day a young studio head named Walt Disney visited Nelbert at her art institute. Walt had a dream to do something that everyone thought was impossible: create a fully animated feature film. But he knew his Animators needed to become better artists before his dream could be realized. While the men who ran the other art schools in town laughed at Walt, Nelbert was fearless. She told him, "Mr. Disney, I believe you can establish a great art form with your animation. Bring your Animators to my school and I will train them to be true artists."

Walt regularly drove his Animators to the Chouinard Art Institute, where Nelbert's teachers helped improve their animation skills so *Snow White and the Seven Dwarfs* could become an artistic masterpiece. Walt was so inspired by Nelbert that he established his own training program at his studio; over the years, many Disney artists graduated from, or taught at, Nelbert's school. Later, when she grew too old to run her school, Walt Disney continued Nelbert's dream of arts education by transforming the Chouinard Art Institute into the California Institute of the Arts. Today the dream Nelbert Chouinard and Walt Disney shared continues at "CalArts," where many of the world's best artists and Animators are taught!

With a *Great mentor* to guide and to teach, the farthest *star* is well within reach.

Marge Champion

(1919–)

An Animated Dance Legend

How do you express yourself? When Great Girl Marge Champion danced, she was one of the first to express movement to help Animators understand their subjects.

As a young girl, Marge often assisted her father in his dance studio. Every dancer in Hollywood studied at her father's studio—even the most popular screen star of the day, Shirley Temple. Marge worked hard and demonstrated dances in each one of her father's classes. One day, Walt Disney called her father, looking for a dancer who could help his artists understand movement and improve their animation. Marge went with several of her father's top dancers to audition. And thanks to her hard work, she got the part!

Marge regularly went to Walt Disney's studio and worked with the artists. She wore a costume and acted out each scene in the film they were creating, *Snow White and the Seven Dwarfs*. As a dancer, Marge understood the movements the Animators were looking for—hand gestures, reactions, dancing, quick steps—and she brought these ideas to life. Marge's action helped the Animators understand what it looked like to call into a wishing well, run through a frightening forest, or joyfully dance as one of the Seven Dwarfs.

After *Snow White* was a success, Marge returned to Walt Disney's studio to create the movements for the Blue Fairy from *Pinocchio*. Her choreography also inspired the artists to animate a chorus of dancing hippos, ostriches, and alligators in *Fantasia*.

Marge continued to express herself through dance all her life. After her work in animation, she had a successful career dancing with her husband, Gower Champion. They starred in movie musicals, had their own television show, danced on Broadway, and toured across the country in the 1940s and 1950s. Marge and Gower included the talented performer Harry Belafonte in their tours and challenged race barriers by featuring this remarkable African American entertainer. Together, they toured throughout the segregated South during the mid-1950s and helped bridge differences for their audiences when they saw these three friends sing and perform together.

Performing and breaking barriers remained a large part of Marge's life. After her husband passed away, Marge continued to perform on Broadway and won an Emmy Award for her choreography on television. After many stage performances, Marge continued dancing and being honored well into her nineties!

Whether *dancing, singing,* or *writing a play,* Great Girls create in their own *special way.*

Hazel Sewell

(1898–1975)

The Artistry of Ink & Paint

What can we do to make something better?
When Hazel Sewell applied her talents, this
Girl Greatly improved Walt Disney's animation.

Hazel was the oldest of ten children growing up in Idaho. She later moved with her husband and young daughter to Hollywood, where they lived in the same neighborhood as Walt Disney's uncle Robert. Hazel met Walt when he first arrived in Hollywood, and used her vast talents to make cartoons with him in his uncle's garage.

When Walt and Roy started their studio in 1923, Hazel continued to help out from time to time. When their studio expanded in 1927, Hazel took charge of the Blackeners who inked the drawings, and became the first woman to run a major department in animation. She trained her teams to improve their skills as they defined the Animators' lines on the front of each cel with ink, and painted on the back of the cel in black, white, and gray to complete each character. Hazel's artists went from just filling in the lines to being the world's best Inkers and Painters.

In 1932, Hazel introduced something different: *COLOR!* Thanks to a new film process that would accurately convey all colors instead of only black, white, and gray, Hazel and her artists could now paint with a wide range of hues. On the animated Silly Symphony short *Flowers and Trees*, Hazel explored how eighty different colors would work together to beautifully paint the story of trees with human qualities. Now vibrant flowers could dance, green trees could sing, and a colorful rainbow could be featured in all its glory. Thanks to Hazel's leadership, the women artists who inked and painted the colorful cels on *Flowers and Trees* at Disney won the first Academy Award® ever given for animation.

Hazel and her teams expanded the palette of colors and artistry in animation. Through Hazel's guidance, the artists of Ink & Paint made the characters memorable and the world of *Snow White and the Seven Dwarfs* believable: there was delicate yellow for Snow White's skirt, dark purple for the Queen's robes, russet browns for the Dwarfs' jackets, and ruby red for the Witch's tempting apple. This film forever changed the movies and was honored with a very special Oscar® statue (that was accompanied by seven little statuettes).

With this legendary movie, Hazel became the first woman to receive a credit as an Art Director within animation. After *Snow White and the Seven Dwarfs*, she retired from animation, but in just ten years, Hazel Sewell advanced the quality and artistry of the final artwork we see on-screen, and forever changed Disney animation.

By improving the *quality* of work that we do, *Great Girls* accomplish so much that is new.

Mary Weiser

(1911–1975)

... and Her Perfect Paints

Have you ever had a problem that needed to be solved? One of the Great Girls of Disney's Ink & Paint Department found the solution to a persistent paint problem.

Walt Disney's animation was created with the cel animation process. Thousands of clear celluloid sheets were inked and painted each day by hundreds of artists. The artists had to work fast, but often the production was slowed down because there were problems with the different kinds of paint they were using.

The Ink & Paint Department used paints that were made for other uses, like painting houses or furniture. These different paints wouldn't mix together or stay on the cels. Often, the paint was lumpy or wouldn't dry evenly. Some colors faded, cracked, and flaked off the cels before they could be photographed. These problems slowed down production and even damaged the cels. In 1935, a talented painter at Disney Studios named Mary Weiser knew she could solve this problem. Mary went to her supervisor, Hazel Sewell, and said, "Let me learn everything I can about paint, and we can make this animation better."

Mary studied chemistry and learned about color, light, paint, dyes, and pigments. She visited factories where paint was made and examined everything she could there. Weiser then came back to Disney Studios and set up the world's first paint laboratory to create special paints for cel animation. Mary's lab was stocked with beakers, thermometers, test tubes, goggles, scales, and masks. She also trained other artists at the Disney Studios' Ink & Paint Department to be paint chemists and technicians.

Mary and her team of women chemists researched, experimented, developed, and tested their paints and created new formulas, concoctions, and solutions. Would they work? Could they mix and blend? Would the colors stay true—even after a great span of time? Ultimately, Mary and her team created paints for Disney animation that met an array of requirements and expanded the department's color selection from 80 shades to over 1,500!

Mary also created a special way to add a rosy glow to Snow White's cheeks called "the Blend." Mary's "Blend" idea was so successful that she received two patents for her invention of this new animation technique. With all her smarts and artistry, Mary and her "perfect paints" forever changed the look of our favorite Disney animated stories.

Mary Weiser's

her name,

and as her story implies,

a

Great Girl

improves things,

if she *wisely* tries!

Kae Sumner

(1916–1996)

"Six Foot Three— What Will It Be?"

Have you ever felt like you don't "fit in"? That was the challenge Great Girl Kae Sumner faced and overcame.

Ever since she was a young girl, Kae was the tallest person in her class. She couldn't hide her height, so Kae stood straight and tall for everyone to see, even though she often bumped into things. Kae's bright smile and sense of humor helped, and she was very popular. But with no one to look at eye-to-eye, Kae sometimes felt lonely.

As Kae grew to six foot three, her artistic skills grew as well. Kae studied, trained, and sharpened her talents to become a very fine artist; and though jobs were hard to find during the Great Depression, Kae took her portfolio to Walt Disney's Hyperion Studio, where Hazel Sewell quickly hired her to work in the Ink & Paint Department.

The workmen at the Studio made a special desk for

Kae that fit her just right so she could paint cels along with the other artists. Soon she mastered the artistry of special effects painting. Kae's talents shined and when the newspapers heard about her artistry on *Snow White and the Seven Dwarfs*, she became famous as "the giant girl who painted Walt's seven little men."

Kae wrote a funny newspaper story about herself and the challenges she had with her height titled "Six Foot Three—What Will It Be?" Everyone loved her article, and soon she received phone calls from other tall people who understood Kae's experiences. At last Kae met eight new friends she could look in the eye!

Tip Toppers

Kae Sumner

Kae and her new friends started a club called the Tip Toppers. When she wasn't painting for Disney animation, Kae and her tall friends would go dancing or bowling together. *Life* magazine featured Kae's story, and soon she was receiving letters and phone calls from tall people in other countries who wanted to start their own clubs.

Kae later became the founder of the International Tall Person's clubs, and some of Kae's clubs are still around today! All over the world, women five feet ten and taller, as well as men at least six feet two, can meet other tall peers and know they are not alone, thanks to this Great Girl of Disney animation.

When we learn
to turn
life's little
"
wrongs
"
"
rights.
"
into
as Kae's story proves,
Great Girls reach
new
heights!

Sylvia Holland

(1900–1974)

Designing Magical Stories

Have you ever turned your ideas into something special? Disney artist Sylvia Holland was a Great Girl whose ideas were not like anyone else's!

Sylvia Holland was a very talented artist and musician who grew up in Winchester, England, and loved cats. As a young woman, Sylvia became an associate of the Royal Institute of British Architects before moving to Canada with her husband, their daughter, and their kitties. At that time, Sylvia was the only woman working as a professional architect in the entire country of Canada!

Sadly, Sylvia's husband passed away before their second child was born, so she moved her young family to Hollywood. With her talent, Sylvia found work as a sketch artist, designing sets for the movies. When she took her daughter to see *Snow White and the Seven Dwarfs*, Sylvia knew she wanted to work at Disney Studios.

And in 1938, Sylvia began doing just that, working with Walt Disney as a Story

Concept Artist, where her artwork showed the other artists and Animators how the story would be told, what it should look like, what colors to use, and how to set the mood or tone of each scene. Sylvia believed "certain cartoon figures [would] become more natural in women artists' hands. Certainly, the women in the audience prefer them that way."

One day, Walt imagined sprites and falling leaves for his musical film *Fantasia*. When the male artists weren't interested in this story, Sylvia was given the job. With her artistic and musical talents, Sylvia created such stunning story ideas filled with enchanted fairies that Walt trusted her with the entire sequence set to Tchaikovsky's "Dance of the Flowers." She also designed the movie's Beethoven's "Pastoral Symphony" segment. Sylvia's clever ideas and artwork clearly showed the other artists at Disney Studios just how magical *Fantasia* would finally be.

Sylvia continued with her artwork while she raised her children and cared for her cats. She later explored characters, colors, and story ideas for other films at Disney Studios, including *Bambi* and *Make Mine Music*. Walt admired Sylvia's artwork, saying she was "a highly talented artist who contributed to the good taste and beauty of our pictures."

With **ideas, talent**, and **hard work**, too, there's no limit to all **Great Girls** can do!

Mildred Rossi

(1915–1998)

(Also known as Milicent Patrick)

Happy with Her Monsters

Where does your imagination take you?
A talented Animator named Mildred
imagined different kinds of characters
for Walt Disney's films.

Mildred was a very imaginative child. When she was a toddler, Mildred's father moved her family around South America while he designed buildings. She spent time exploring, imagining, sketching, and designing alongside her father. Her family ultimately moved to Northern California, where her father was a structural engineer working for Julia Morgan—the noted architect who designed Hearst Castle. Mildred admired Julia and watched carefully as the castle Julia was building took form.

Upon graduating from high school, Mildred studied art at a local college before she received a scholarship to attend the legendary Chouinard Art Institute in Los Angeles. After Mildred completed her training, her talents took her to Walt Disney's studio, where she was one of the first women animators on his movies.

Working in the Studio's "Rainbow Room," Mildred designed and mixed the beautiful colors in Disney's animation. She moved into Special Effects Animation and became a Lead Animator within Color Animation, applying her imagination and talent to *Fantasia*. Mildred created the beautiful color animation for the segment of the movie set to Bach's "Toccata and Fugue in D Minor," and helped the fairies of the Tchaikovsky's "Dance of the Flowers" segment add frost to the leaves of the forest.

The evil creature Chernabog from the "Night on Bald Mountain" scene was especially challenging. Walt wanted to show how this scary monster could be defeated by light, but wasn't sure how to do this. Using her imagination, Mildred worked with chalk pastels and found a colorful solution to the problem. By adding a bright shade to the dark monster frame by frame, Mildred created the look of a light shining on and off the creature, defeating Chernabog's evil force with the dawn of a new day. Mildred's artistic talents helped make Walt Disney's musical experiment, *Fantasia*, a masterpiece!

Chernabog wasn't the only creature Mildred created. She went on to become the first woman to design famous Hollywood monsters! In fact, she created many creepy characters for Hollywood films, including a wolf man, mutant bugs from outer space, and a gilled man who was half human and half fish. This character lived in a dark lagoon and fell in love with a beautiful girl. "These creatures grow on a sketch board in front of me," Mildred said. "I'm happy with my monsters." Many years later, filmmakers continue to be inspired by—and audiences still marvel at—Mildred's marvelous monsters.

Great Girls *imagine* the most marvelous things, from monsters to dewdrops on fairies' wings.

Gyo Fujikawa

(1908–1998)

Illustrator Extraordinaire!

Have you ever overcome something difficult to accomplish something special? Great Girl Gyo Fujikawa used her talents to create positive change.

Gyo was a wonderful artist who loved to paint and draw all that she saw around her. Growing up in California, Gyo remembered, "Instead of playing with dolls and toys, I'd try to sketch flowers and animals. Even then I seemed to know what I wanted to be when I grew up." Gyo knew that talent was only part of her story: "It takes a lot of hard work, determination, and sincerity to succeed."

A teacher in high school recognized Gyo's talent and helped her get a scholarship at the Chouinard Art Institute, where she studied drawing, painting, design, and layout. After completing school, Gyo began working at Walt Disney's studio in the Advertising Art Department. She designed books, fabrics, plates, and figurines featuring all the characters within *Fantasia*. Gyo's artistry also helped introduce classical music to people all over the world.

Gyo then moved to New York City to work as a Lead Artist within the Disney products division. But after the bombing of Pearl Harbor in 1941, which led to America's entrance into World War II, Gyo faced injustice due to her heritage. Her parents and siblings in California were uprooted and forced to move to a relocation camp in Arkansas because they were Japanese. Walt visited Gyo in New York and made sure she was all right during this difficult time.

After the war, Gyo continued drawing and creating advertising artwork for other companies. She lived in New York with her two poodles, Suzu and Kiku, who were often seen in her artwork. Soon she began writing and illustrating children's books and was one of the first American artists to include children of many different races in her artwork. She worked hard and created more than fifty books that were translated into many languages so children and their parents around the world could read them.

Gyo later designed postage stamps for the U.S. Postal Service. Her first stamp celebrated the friendship between the United States and Japan, and another celebrated the Beautification of America campaign. Thanks to her diligence and talent, Gyo was invited to the White House, where President Lyndon Johnson and his wife, Lady Bird Johnson, personally congratulated her. "It was very exciting," Gyo said. "I am very proud to make a small contribution to enhance the daily lives of all Americans."

Many of the
Great Girls
of Disney
animation
soared
beyond the
clouds!

Have you ever dreamed of doing something that seemed impossible? These Great Girls of Disney animation accomplished the "seemingly impossible" within the world of aviation.

Mary Goodrich

(1907–2004)

First to the Skies

Mary Goodrich was an adventurous young girl who loved to read stories and dreamed of being a journalist. But after Charles Lindbergh became the first to fly solo across the Atlantic Ocean in May of 1927, Mary also became interested in flying. The first time she rode in an airplane, she recalled, "It was the most unusual experience of my life. I fell in love with being up in the air."

When Mary applied for a job at the local newspaper to become a reporter, the editor laughed and said, "It's unlikely because we don't hire girls. But if you become a pilot, we'll hire you." In 1929, both of her dreams came true: Mary became the first woman in the state of Connecticut to earn her pilot's license—and soon after became a journalist. Mary was the first female reporter in the history of her newspaper—and in the nation—to have a regular aviation column with her name on it.

Mary bought her own airplane—a Fairchild KR-21 single engine biplane—and was soon competing in air shows and races. She would often fly low over her parents' house and yell, "I'll be home soon for dinner!" The neighbors would look up at passing planes and say, "There goes Mary Goodrich!"

That same year, Mary helped start the Ninety-Nines, one of the first organizations for women pilots. The legendary pilot Amelia Earhart was even a member! Mary also flew along with many women pilots in the Betsy Ross Corps, which helped provide aid and relief during times of national emergencies and in defense of the United States. Mary traveled across the Atlantic Ocean on the famous *Hindenburg* blimp and later became the first woman to fly solo to Cuba.

When Mary's eyesight began to change, however, she could no longer be a pilot, so she continued with her writing and went to work at the Disney Studios. While there, Mary started the Story Research Department. She worked closely with the writers to research ideas and characters and explore how they could be made into animated movies. Mary and her teams helped shape the stories of such Disney films as *Bambi* and *Dumbo*—the tale of an unlikely elephant who also learned to fly!

Grace Huntington

(1913–1948)

Let Me Fly!

When Grace Huntington was a little girl, she loved stories such as *Peter Pan,* the tale of a boy who could fly, among others. "I read Jules Verne's *From the Earth to the Moon,*" Grace remembered. "That book left me with an unquenchable desire to someday, in some way, bring the dream of a trip through space a little closer to reality."

Grace's love for stories continued as she grew. After she graduated from school, she was hired as one of the first female writers at Disney Studios. Grace worked hard at perfecting her craft and soon became one of the first women to write for the early Disney short cartoons. Often the only woman at story meetings, Grace fearlessly presented her ideas and acted them out for Walt Disney and the artists. "I began to learn the lessons that were necessary. . . . The first was to get over whatever shyness I possessed. I found that it was not only fun, but that it was going to mean a lot to me later . . . in every situation I might have to face." Grace's concepts became a part of the animated Mickey and Minnie Mouse films, as well as the Silly Symphonies.

While Grace worked hard at Disney animation, she also loved to fly. Her brother was a pilot with a small airplane, a Fairchild 24 named *The Blue Dragon*. Grace trained with *The Blue Dragon* and soon became a licensed pilot. Grace flew every chance she got, and the higher she soared, the happier she was.

She remembered her childhood dream of taking a trip through space, which ignited her desire to be the first woman to fly a small airplane higher than anyone had ever flown one before. To accomplish this, she studied and practiced. It was difficult; many pilots wouldn't help her because she was a girl, but Grace's dream was important to her—and she persisted. Grace found a teacher who believed in what she was trying to achieve, and he helped her train.

Then, in 1939, on a beautiful sunny day in Burbank, California, Grace flew a sleek, all-black Taylorcraft plane with red trimmings, which she nicknamed Black Beauty. Because she was flying at such a high altitude, she wore an oxygen mask and bundled up in warm clothes. "I took off as soon as possible," Grace said. "Before I was past the tower, my altimeter read one thousand feet and I was still going up like an elevator." Higher and higher, Grace climbed, rising to ten thousand feet . . . then fifteen thousand . . . and soon twenty thousand feet. Suddenly, there was a loud *boom!* Was it the engine? Did a cable break? Was she in danger? Would she have to give up on her dream?

"The trouble was easily discovered," Grace remembered. "The windshield had cracked!" Because Grace flew so high, the air temperature had suddenly grown colder outside her plane. "It was twelve degrees below zero outside," said Grace, "and the wind had been blowing in through the cracked windshield." But Grace kept control of the plane and bravely continued to climb higher.

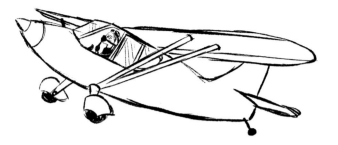

Grace's altimeter stopped working at 22,750 feet; yet she continued flying higher than she had ever flown before. "I stayed until I knew I had just enough gas to get back to the field and then started down," Grace said.

Reporters and journalists waited on the ground. Once Grace landed, the reporters and photographers quickly asked their questions: "How cold was it up there?" "It was eighty-four degrees on the ground when I took off," Grace replied. "Twelve below zero at the top." Even though she was back on the ground, Grace still shivered in her heavy flight suit.

"How long did it take you to make the flight?" "Two hours going up and thirty-five minutes coming down!"

Then the most important question was asked: "How high did you fly?" Since some of Grace's equipment had stopped working in-flight, she responded, "The altimeter registered 22,750 feet." But when Grace's barograph was later calibrated in Washington, D.C., it was officially declared that Grace had set the *national altitude* record for a female pilot in a lightplane by soaring to 24,310.975 feet!

As a woman in the 1930s, Grace accomplished something that had never been done before. Rocket ships traveling "from the Earth to the moon" were later explored in the 1960s, thanks to the early exploits of people like Grace, who fulfilled her dream of flying through space, high above the world. Through all that she accomplished in aviation, Grace still remembered her time writing at the Disney Studios: "Every quality I was developing then would make me a better person and a better pilot."

Elizabeth Chambers (1920–1961)

In Service to Her Country

Elizabeth "Betty" Chambers was a young artist who worked at Walt Disney's studio. She carefully trained and worked hard as an Inker on the animated shorts and feature films. Betty's beautiful artistry helped create many of the memorable characters from such films as *Pinocchio, Fantasia, Bambi*, and *Dumbo*.

Betty was married to a young pilot, and she, like him, loved to fly. Betty wanted to get her pilot's license, but was delayed in that pursuit when she gave birth to a baby boy. When World War II started, Betty's husband learned about the WASP program, which stood for Women Airforce Service Pilots. Female pilots were trained to transport planes so more male pilots could serve in combat. The artists at Disney designed the Fifinella logo for these brave pilots who flew aircraft and materials for U.S. troops.

Betty's husband knew she would be a perfect candidate and wanted her to become a WASP. "I love flying as he did," Betty said. "He wanted me to fly. . . . In fact, he wanted to teach me, but it didn't work out that way." Sadly, her husband was killed during the war. Betty's parents helped take care of her son while she moved to Avenger Field in Texas and trained to become a

WASP. "I hope to be able to replace a man to do the job that my husband wanted to do," Betty said.

As a former Disney artist, Betty wore her "Fifi" logo proudly and soon earned her wings. Betty became one of the first pilots in the WASP program and the only recent widow and mother who served her country as such. She continued special training at different airfields, with over 420 hours of flight time. Betty bravely flew transport missions during the war and piloted many different types of planes.

After the war, Betty continued to fly as an airline pilot at a time when there weren't very many women pilots. Nearly thirty-five years after these brave female pilots served their country as civilians in the WASP program, they were finally recognized as veterans, and in 2009, President Barack Obama gave each of the WASP flyers the Congressional Gold Medal.

When *Great Girls* set their minds to a plan,

their *dreams take flight,* and they prove they can!

Mary Blair

(1911–1978)

Color Designer Extraordinaire

What's your favorite color? Mary Blair's favorite colors made her one of the Greatest Girls of animation.

Mary always saw the world in a colorful way. Her talents mixing teals and tan tones helped her win a national art contest while still in high school. In art school, Mary met another talented artist named Lee Blair. Together Mary and Lee created art and painted with the vibrant colors of love. After they were married, the Blairs continued to paint and sketch together. But during the Great Depression's grip, people weren't buying artwork, so they applied their talents to Disney animation.

During World War II, Walt Disney planned a goodwill tour to South America with a small group of his top artists to share the magic of animation. The idea of touring the vibrant cultures and scenery of these places appealed to Mary, so she asked Walt if she could join her husband. Soon Mary was flying across Latin America.

Travel opened Mary's eyes to different shades and styles. She collected crisp colors from Cuba, expanded her palette in Peru, mixed magnificent magentas from Mexico, found new hues of blues from the shores of Argentina, and brought a bounty of browns and berries back from Brazil. Colors that were blended with Mary's brushes came out more bright and colorful than ever! Mary painted everything she saw, capturing new pigments and applying them to her artwork.

Mary's Latin American adventures came to life in *Saludos Amigos* and *The Three Caballeros.* These films led to many other movies at Disney Studios. Mary blended rosy pinks with indigo blues into the magical world of *Cinderella.* She mixed enchanted corals, crimsons, and cyans to define the world of the Queen of Hearts in *Alice in Wonderland*. And she designed a colorful adventure of leafy greens and fantastic fuchsias to bring *Peter Pan*'s Never Land adventures to vibrant life.

Mary had new colors to explore, so she left Disney Studios and moved to New York. There, she began creating colorful campaigns for advertisements, illustrated children's books, and designed sets for TV commercials and movies. With all these new shades added to her palette, Mary later returned to design many other projects with Walt Disney . . . but that's another colorful adventure!

Mary Costa

(1930–)

The Voice of a Princess

Where will your dreams and talents take you? Great Girl Mary Costa traveled the world once she learned to make her dreams come true.

Walt Disney was working on his latest animated movie, *Sleeping Beauty*. He wanted this to be spectacular, so the voice of Princess Aurora needed to be very special. Even though his film had been in production for several years, Walt Disney still hadn't found the voice of the princess.

One day, a talented young singer named Mary Costa came to Walt Disney's studio to audition. Walt Disney listened to Mary speak from behind a screen so he could use his imagination. When Walt heard her sing, he knew he had found Princess Aurora! Walt told her, "When you get in front of that microphone . . . use all the colors of your vocal palette and paint with your voice."

"Singing was my most personal way of expressing myself," said Mary. She dreamed of being a great opera singer, and Walt Disney encouraged her. "He always said to me, 'If you have

the four "D's"—Dedication, Determination, and Discipline—you'll achieve your Dreams!'" She remembered Walt's words when she established her career within the grand world of opera.

With dedicated determination and discipline, Mary worked hard at singing with all the colors of her voice, and focused on her dream. With her beautiful soprano, Mary performed with the Metropolitan Opera in New York and the San Francisco Opera in California, singing the lead roles from such operas as *La Bohème* and *La Traviata*. Soon she was performing all around the world in the great opera houses of Paris, London, Milan, Moscow, Tokyo, and more, delighting audiences wherever she sang!

President John F. Kennedy and his wife, Jackie, followed Mary's career. When the president died in 1963, Mrs. Kennedy requested that Mary perform at his funeral. Mary was deeply honored. Her vocal tribute to the fallen president was telecast around the world.

Mary sang on television, performed in movies, and received many honors. When she retired from singing, Mary found a new dream: President George W. Bush asked her to serve on the president's National Council on the Arts. "This is a wonderful chance for me to give back to others a portion of that which was so generously given to me," Mary said. Remembering Walt's four "D's," Mary worked to make sure children all over the country could learn more about the arts and discover their own talents.

Great Girls

know

with whatever you do,

apply the

four D's

to make

dreams

come true.

To tell animated tales, specific artists draw the movement of each character— the Animators!

BIRDS

TINKER BELL

Do you know of a change that is overdue? For many years, people thought girls couldn't animate, but many Great Girls proved they could.

Retta Scott

(1916–1990)

She Had a Feeling for Power

Retta stood out as a special artist during her time at the Chouinard Art Institute. "I loved to draw animals," Retta recalled, "and spent much time doing this at the old Griffith Park Zoo" in Los Angeles. Before she graduated, Retta started working at Disney Studios in the Story Department. "I began to work on *Bambi*." Retta noted when reflecting on the tale of a young deer finding his place within the world, "I was delighted with the work." Retta's pieces were so strong that she began working as an Inbetweener, creating drawings between the Lead Animators' works on several scenes. In an early story meeting, Walt Disney took note of Retta's sketches.

Retta was tasked with animating a challenging sequence for *Bambi*. "I developed the hunting dogs into vicious, snarling, really mean beasts," Retta remembered. "My first test was used for the picture. I was so pleased! I estimated that during that year I had drawn over fifty-six thousand dogs for *Bambi*!" Retta became the first woman to receive a credit as an Animator on a Disney film, and she continued animating on many of the military training films created at Disney Studios to help Allied soldiers throughout World War II. After the success of her powerful drawings at Disney, Retta animated at many other studios. Just like Bambi finding his way, Retta found her place within the world of animation!

Berta "Bea" Tamargo

(1926–)

A Multitalented Artist

Born in Havana, Cuba, "Bea" was a talented young violinist. But when her family came to America, Bea's interest in fine art grew, and soon she turned in her violin bow for a paintbrush.

After completing school, Bea was hired within the Disney Ink & Paint Department, where she quickly mastered the fine art of inking. Bea's talents were strong, and soon she put down her pen and picked up a pencil to work as an Assistant Animator. Bea worked on *Cinderella, Alice in Wonderland,* and *Peter Pan.* While she was animating on *Lady and the Tramp,* Bea officially became a U.S. citizen.

With her tiny size, Bea also provided live-action reference work for characters in different Disney films. Her Cuban heritage was often brought into service as she interpreted for visiting dignitaries and translated many of Walt Disney's cartoons into Spanish. Between films, Bea often took her brushes, pens, and pencils to the beach, where she would paint and sketch nature and revel in her love of art.

Rae Medby

(1917–2002)

"Rosie" with a Pencil

Born in Norway, Rae traveled with her family to the United States when she was a young girl. This smart and talented artist stayed focused on her goals all through school. Rae delivered her graduation valedictorian speech, and the very next day moved to Los Angeles to try out at Disney Studios. Rae was the strongest painter in her training class, and she was hired to paint and ink on the earliest Disney animated features, including *Snow White and the Seven Dwarfs, Pinocchio, Fantasia,* and *Bambi.*

Meanwhile, with many of the men fighting in World War II, a number of women took over their jobs. "Rosie the Riveter" became the nickname for these ladies, who traded their skirts for dungarees and took the place of men who had joined the military. They worked in the factories producing war supplies and kept other vital industries going. This was also true of the women at Disney Studios. Dozens of Great Girls, including Sylvia Niday, Phyllis Mooney, and Lula Drake-Jekel—along with Rae herself—trained to become Animators so the Studio could continue making movies. And Rae found great success doing so! She became one of two artists assigned to work with noted film director Frank Capra on a famous series of documentaries about the war.

Rae continued animating for the military units and was so dedicated, she also trained to be a "Sky Watcher." This meant Rae volunteered to identify aircraft and track airplane activity. Rae was one of many Great Girls who bravely applied their animation talents and helped win the war.

Retta Davidson

(1921–1998)

Training New Animators

Ever since she was a little girl, Retta had always wanted to be an art teacher. She was thrilled to be hired as a Painter on *Pinocchio* when she was only seventeen! With her positive attitude and sense of humor, Retta loved to help others. She soon became a Special Effects Painter on *Fantasia* and *Bambi,* and as such, Retta was part of the first set of Great Girls from the Ink & Paint Department to be trained as Animators. She was one of three artists who made the cut, but left to serve her country as a draftsman and a projectionist overseeing the navy's film library in Washington, D.C.

After the war, Retta returned to the Animation Department at Disney Studios, where she worked for over two decades. In all these years, she took some time off to have two children and to earn her degree in art education. After animating commercials and movies at other studios, Retta's dream of being an art teacher was realized when she became one of the leading animation

teachers in Canada, teaching students who had no experience with making their artwork move.

In 1982, when she was a grandmother, the Disney Studios brought Retta back to train a new group of Animators. "This has always been my home," Retta said. Her return gave her a chance "to repay the Studio for the years of early training I received in the golden years." Retta continued working at Disney while she enjoyed being a grandmother and teaching the next generation of artists. Retta truly opened new opportunities for more Great Girls of animation!

With

pencils,

pens & *brushes,*

plus pure

imagination,

Great Girls

will always create

great

animation!

Time Line

1901
Walt Disney is born.

1923
Walt makes his first Alice Comedy—*Alice's Wonderland*—in Kansas City, Missouri.

1923
Walt and his brother Roy establish the first animation studio in Hollywood.

1925
Couples Walt & Lillian and Roy & Edna marry.

1937
Snow White and the Seven Dwarfs opens and later receives a special Honorary Academy Award®.

1940
Pinocchio and *Fantasia* both debut.

1941
Dumbo is released, and the United States enters World War II.

1942
Bambi premieres.

1950
Cinderella debuts.

1951
Alice in Wonderland arrives in theaters.

1953
Peter Pan successfully soars to new heights.

1955
Lady and the Tramp bounds into theaters.

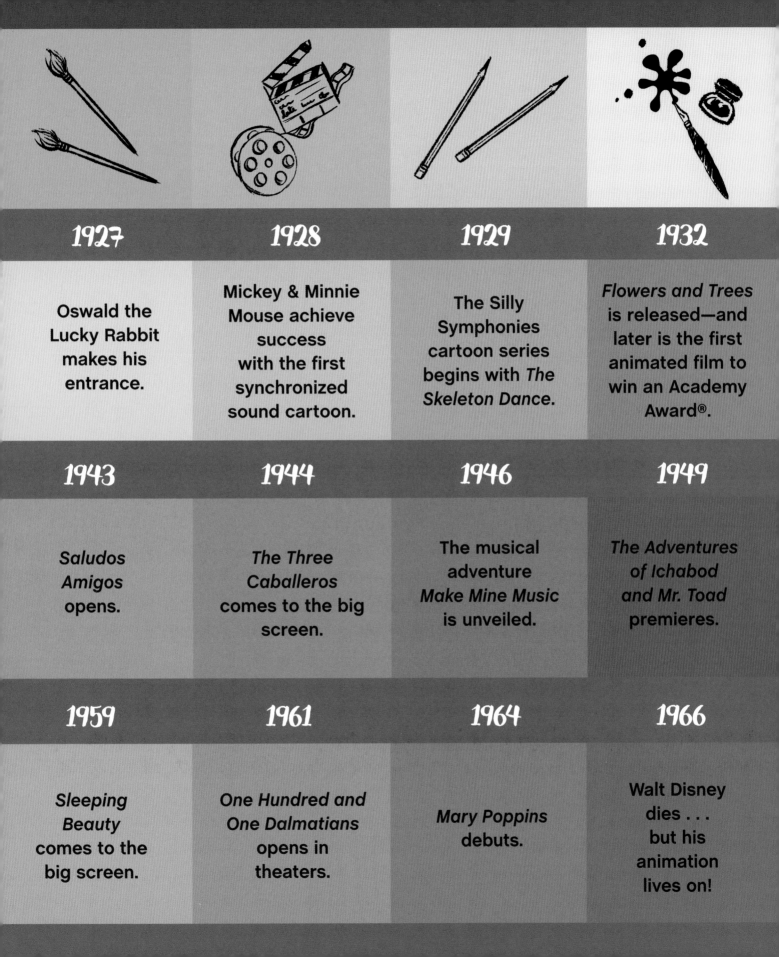

1927	1928	1929	1932
Oswald the Lucky Rabbit makes his entrance.	Mickey & Minnie Mouse achieve success with the first synchronized sound cartoon.	The Silly Symphonies cartoon series begins with *The Skeleton Dance*.	*Flowers and Trees* is released—and later is the first animated film to win an Academy Award®.

1943	1944	1946	1949
Saludos Amigos opens.	*The Three Caballeros* comes to the big screen.	The musical adventure *Make Mine Music* is unveiled.	*The Adventures of Ichabod and Mr. Toad* premieres.

1959	1961	1964	1966
Sleeping Beauty comes to the big screen.	*One Hundred and One Dalmatians* opens in theaters.	*Mary Poppins* debuts.	Walt Disney dies . . . but his animation lives on!

How Animation Is Made

Animation is an art form that involves many artists contributing their talents to tell a story. Walt Disney's animation was created through the "cel animation" process. Today the technology is different, but many of the roles involved in animation are still the same:

WRITERS AND RESEARCHERS find and create the stories that will be told.

STORY ARTISTS expand the story with small drawings that visually tell the tale. These drawings are displayed on large storyboards so all the artists understand what will happen.

CONCEPT ARTISTS explore visual ideas and styles for the look of the animation.

VOICE AND REFERENCE ACTORS provide the voices for the characters, as well as movement ideas for the Animators.

ANIMATORS draw the movements of the characters to tell the stories. Other artists help the Lead Animator, including **Assistant Animators**, who continue the Animator's vision; "**Inbetweeners**," who add drawings between the work of the Lead Animators; and **Cleanup Artists**, who finalize each drawing so the lines are clean and defined.

Great Girls of animation understand each role.

COLOR ARTISTS work in the **Paint Labs,** where all the vibrant, colorful paint is created. Today color is applied digitally. **Color Model Supervisors** design the final colors for each character.

INK & PAINT ARTISTS transfer the Animators' drawings onto thousands of clear celluloid sheets. During the early years, **Inkers** redrew the Animators' pencil lines onto the front of the cels with ink pens; then the **Painters** carefully painted all the colors on the backside of the cels with paintbrushes. Today this is accomplished digitally.

SPECIAL EFFECTS involves a wide range of artists who create various unusual elements such as fog, smoke, fire, and even pixie dust on-screen.

BACKGROUNDS are created by artists who paint the environments where each part of the story takes place.

CAMERA OPERATORS photograph the cels frame by frame against a colorful background onto film. Today final images are digitally recorded.

COMPOSERS write the music within a film to help support the story.

EDITORS cut the film segments together, and **Music Editors** add the recorded music to complete the final film.

For it takes many hands to achieve one goal.

Acknowledgments

Within this volume

that you *behold*

are *stories long hidden*,

now *finally* told.

Should these pages *inspire*

what you one day *create*,

thank these *talented people*

whose efforts were *GREAT* ...

To the many Great Girls within this volume, and their families, who shared their remarkable stories! Brittany Rubiano & Wendy Lefkon for your keen editorial talents, belief, and valued efforts in sharing these hidden stories! Lorelay Bové for brilliantly capturing the spirit of these Great Girls with your sublime artistry! Winnie Ho for the beautiful design to express these Great stories within. Grace Lee for your magnificent art management. Monica Vasquez for Greatly keeping this all on track. Becky Cline & Mike Buckhoff for your valued archival support, and finally, Joe Campana for your valiant ancestral sleuthing!

—*Mindy Johnson*

Thanks for letting me be part of capturing the history of these great ladies of Disney Animation. It's an honor to be part of this amazing book full of inspiration!

—*Lorelay Bové*